Reiki Wings
Student Notes
Usui Reiki
Level I

Disclaimer

The Reiki Wings Teacher's Handbook and accompanying Student Notes are intended to be used as a teaching support by a Usui Reiki Master/Teacher who has completed their training and attunements with a qualified Usui Reiki Master/Teacher. This text is not meant to replace any training process provided by a qualified teacher.

The information, suggestions, and exercises contained in this book are for the purposes of education only. There is no intention of medical diagnosis or advice. The reader must seek medical advice in matters involving health related issues. The author shall not be liable nor responsible for any person using these notes as a self-healing tool.

The author has made every effort to relate accurate website information at the time of publishing. Therefore, there is no assumption of responsibility for changes made to any information source after the date of publication.

For more information contact Reiki Associates:
613-264-8165
www.reikiassociates.com

Design and Production: Reiki Associates
Cover Design: Denise Carpenter
Cover Layout: Mary Ellen Dick
Cover Art: Chris Carpenter
Photographs: Mary Ferguson, and Mary Ellen Dick
Editing: Monika S. Walker
Proofreading: Joffre Carpenter-Ducharme

Usui Reiki Level I, Student Notes
Contents

Introduction to Usui Reiki

What is Reiki?

Reiki is a system of assisting energy movement through the laying on of hands. The form of Reiki we are learning is referred to as *Usui Shiki Ryoho,* which means the "Usui System of Natural Healing". Sensei Mikao Usui made Reiki available in Kyoto, Japan in the early 20th Century. It evolved within and was embraced by a culture that was steeped in respect for *Rei* and *Ki*.

The "ki" in Reiki refers to *Ki* – also known by various names such as *Qi* and *Chi*. *Ki* is recognised throughout the Orient as the energy of life and is the foundation of many ancient practices ranging from Feng Shui and flower arranging to martial arts. It is also central to different spiritual practices and styles of healing such as Mikkyo Buddhism, Kiko, Qigong and Japanese Shintoism. The Japanese character *Ki* can be translated into English as energy, nature scene, talent and feeling.

Rei means universal, holy, spirit, mystery, gift, nature spirit or invisible spirit. When both meanings are combined as the word or character *Reiki*, the meaning becomes, "Spiritually guided life force energy." Although many forms of Reiki have since evolved, the meaning of the Japanese character and the essence of these practices remain the same.

When we practice Reiki, we become a channel for this life energy that is guided by a universal wisdom. Since the energy comes from the universe, it is unlimited. It differs from other forms of energy work in that it does not rely on the wisdom or strength of the practitioner. Our pivotal contribution is ***our willingness or intent***. Our personal request is to have this energy flow through us, ground us, and benefit our recipients. Then, like water through a young bamboo reed, the Reiki will flow.

Reiki is a special technique that can be used by those who have been "attuned" to Reiki energy. The attunement stimulates the student's ever-present energy and initiates their ability to access universal energy through the intention to do so. Anyone of any age can receive an attunement to practice Reiki.

Reiki can be used to treat ourselves, others, our homes, animals, plants, crystals, electronics and the Earth, in fact just about anything! Reiki works in a gentle manner, improving the well-being of the recipient as well as the practitioner.

Reiki works independently of our belief systems. It can be accessed without any background knowledge of psychology, philosophy, religion or medicine, yet can assist people in these and other fields.

The Benefits of Reiki

What are the benefits of Reiki?

- Reiki magnifies inner perception. It helps each of us sharpen our intuition and develop a greater sensitivity to our own energy as well as to the energy of others.

- Reiki promotes self-confidence and a trust in life as a benevolent force.

- Reiki helps us develop more compassion towards everyone and everything.

- Reiki promotes a growing responsibility in each of us for our own life and well-being.

- Reiki helps us solve old problems. During Reiki initiations or treatments, old problems may bubble up in order to be resolved. It is then up to us individually, whether we choose to resolve them.

The History of Usui Reiki

The history of Usui Reiki Ryoho that is taught in the West has gradually unfolded over the years. There are few validated facts regarding Sensei Usui's personal life and many questions have been asked about Mrs. Takata's teachings of him. As the teaching and use of Usui Reiki has grown globally, the East has responded to the need for accurate historical information regarding the history of Reiki in the East and of Sensei Usui's own life history.

What we know.

Mikao Usui was born in the small village of Taniai (now called Miyama cho) in Japan on August 15, 1865. He was born a tendai Buddhist. He was schooled at a Tendai monastery and at a young age, studied Aiki Jutsu and Yagyu Ryu, Japanese martial arts. These practices help the students develop and use their life force energy. Sensei Usui was an avid seeker of spiritual teachings and as such traveled all over Japan, China, and Europe studying medicine, psychology, religion, and spiritual development. He was a member of a metaphysical group called Rei Jyutu Ka while at the same time working at various levels in the government, including a position as secretary to Shinpei Goto, the Governor of the Standard of Railways, who went on to become the mayor of Tokyo. At age 43, he married Sadako Suzuki and together they had two children.

Sensei Usui was disciplined in Shugendo, a Tendai Buddhism meditation practice which requires intensive training. To foster this training, in 1922 he decided to go on a 21-day retreat on Mount Kurama where he would fast and meditate to seek enlightenment. He climbed Mount Kurama and chose a special place for his meditation, facing east. He collected 21 stones and threw one away for every day that passed. For 20 days nothing happened. On the final day of his retreat, while standing under a waterfall, he did a meditation designed to open and purify the Crown Chakra. This caused him to have a spiritual awakening and a powerful understanding of energy. In this state of expanded awareness a great spiritual energy filled his being with clarity. Sensei Usui realised that this energy affected the body on the physical, mental, emotional and spiritual levels.

Sensei Usui moved, with his wife and children, to Tokyo in April, 1922. Based on his lifelong spiritual journey and his more recent spiritual experience, he developed "The Usui System of Natural Healing or Usui Reiki Ryoho Gakkai." Sensei Usui also adapted the five spiritual principles developed by the Meiji Emperor of Japan (1868-1912), guiding people towards a life of compassion for themselves and others in the form of the five precepts or principles which are used to this day in Reiki. Shortly afterward, he opened a clinic in Harajuku and began doing Reiki sessions and teaching classes.

On September 1, 1923, just before noon, the great Kanto earthquake struck and killed over 100,000 people, leaving thousands more injured and homeless. Sensei Usui and his students grieved for their people and decided to take Reiki to the survivors. They worked day and night, giving Reiki to as many as they could. The Meiji Emperor honoured Sensei Usui for his dedication and contribution to their country.

Sensei Usui wanted this simple Reiki energy technique to be available to all people worldwide. In 1925, at the age of 60, he opened a larger clinic in Nakano, and then travelled and lectured until he passed away from a massive stroke on March 9, 1926.

Sensei Usui was buried at Saihoji Temple in Suginami-Ku, Tokyo. With deep gratitude, a large memorial stone was erected by his students, describing his life and work with Reiki. In four short years, he had taught over 2,000 students and trained 16 teachers.

One of these teachers was Sensei Chujiro Hayashi. Sensei Hayashi was a retired Naval Officer and a surgeon. He is credited for the Reiki hand positions we use today. In 1931, Sensei Hayashi founded a Reiki clinic in Tokyo, and it was to this clinic in 1935 that Hawayo Takata, a Japanese-American woman, came to be treated. Hawayo Takata was born in 1900 in Hawaii. In 1935, as a widow raising two active young daughters, she developed asthma and other physical disorders. She was told she needed an operation to save her life and arranged to have surgery while visiting

Japan. On the day set for the operation, Mrs. Takata repeatedly heard the voice of her late husband telling her not to go ahead with the procedure. Full of apprehension, Mrs. Takata asked her doctor if there were any other options for treatment. The doctor recommended a Reiki clinic nearby.

She was skeptical after she received the treatment, and first believed that the heat she experienced through contact with the practitioners' hands had been facilitated by electrical equipment. She checked the room, but found no such equipment. Sensei Hayashi explained his system of Reiki to her and that the heat was generated by the life force energy. Later, freed of her symptoms and impressed by the experience, she approached Sensei Hayashi to ask if he would teach her the technique, explaining that she wanted to take it back to Hawaii with her. Initially she was refused because she was a foreigner. But, during the course of her treatments Sensei Hayashi recanted and accepted her as an apprentice for one year, during which time she was attuned to First and Second Level Reiki.

Mrs. Takata returned home to Hawaii and began giving regular Reiki sessions. Due to the various factors, such as her personality, the political atmosphere of the United States, and her Japanese heritage to name a few, she combined the teachings of Sensei Usui and Sensei Hayashi then made some Western adjustments to produce a more Western practice. Three years later, Sensei Hayashi visited her and she was made a Reiki Master within the Usui Reiki Ryoho System. Over the next 40 years, Mrs. Takata worked diligently to bring Reiki to the Western World. However, it was not until the last 10 years of her life that she began to train other Masters. At the time of her death in 1980, she had initiated 22 Masters. Her granddaughter, Ms. Phyllis Lei Furumoto, was one of those Masters. Ms. Furumoto continued teaching her grandmother's Usui Reiki throughout the Western world.

What is Important.

History has a way of rewriting itself depending on the point of view of the author. As we grow even more rapidly into a global society, with more information being shared, there has been an impact on teachings of the history of Usui Reiki. But, take note that, the updating of the history has not had an impact on the individual student's or teacher's connection with the Reiki Energy regardless of when their training took place. The most important teaching is your direct relationship with the Reiki Energy. It asks for your conscious intent and consistent practice to build and enhance your capacity for direct interaction. As you consciously practice, your relationship will flourish.

Author's Lineage

Sensei Mikao Usui

↓

Sensei Chujiro Hayashi

↓

Hawayo Takata

↓

Phyllis Lei Furumoto

↓

Leah Smith

↓

Denise Carpenter

Create Your Lineage

Sensei
Mikao Usui

Usui Reiki Principles

Usui Reiki Governing Principles

Sensei Usui developed the philosophy that people need to take responsibility for their own lives. This governing foundation includes the importance of asking to receive Reiki and the mutual exchange of energy.

The person must ask.

The recipient must ask to be treated for two reasons. First, we must have the recipient's permission. We must respect the recipient's free will and the choices that come of it. Second, a recipient must be open to receiving Reiki. The simple act of asking helps open the recipient's energy field. When a recipient says, "I want Reiki," they are making a conscious decision to become an active participant, beginning the process to change where they are and to rebalance their physical and emotional state of being. Sometimes a voiceless, yet profound, request for Reiki is made on the soul level. Being attentive to energy and sensations allows Reiki to guide us during these occasions.

There must be an exchange of energy for services.

Reiki energy belongs to the Universe and flows freely. When we value and are mindful of the dynamic, positive flow of energy between people, balance, trust, and optimism can flourish.

To acknowledge the time and intention invested by the practitioner and to prevent indebtedness or dependence, it is encouraged that Reiki be given in exchange for something. This could be in the form of goods, services, or money. The exchange is also reflective of the recipient's investment in the process.

The Five Principles of Usui Reiki

Just for today, do not anger.

Just for today, do not worry.

Just for today, I will live in gratitude.
I will honour myself, my parents, my elders,
and my teachers.

Just for today, I will earn my living honestly.

Just for today, I will be kind to every living thing.

The Five Principles of Usui Reiki

The Meiji Emperor of Japan (1868-1912), who led Japan during Sensei Usui's adulthood, originally gave the five principles as guidelines for a fulfilled life. Sensei Usui adopted and adapted these principles as guidelines for evolving our personal development physically, emotionally and spiritually.

These guidelines all begin with, "Just for today." But, what exactly does this mean? All five principles encourage us to live in the present moment where we can most effectively apply integrity to our actions, leaving yesterday and tomorrow in the care of the universe.

1. Just for today, do not anger.

The ideal being taught is not to suppress anger but to be aware of the emotion and explore it when it arises. Acknowledge, observe and learn the lessons it can provide. "How does it serve me?", "Is it masking a fear?" and "Can I find its path to compassion?" are valuable questions. The use of physical touch and body awareness can also help us get in touch with our feelings.

Some leaders in self-awareness and compassion have devoted a great amount of study to the experience of anger. Reiki encourages our personal development by helping us identify and make peace with our anger. With our determined honesty, the tools provided through these and other techniques, can lead to great personal insight and freedom.

Our growing understanding of ourselves and others allows us to move out of the past more quickly, cease identifying with anger in the immediate situation, and arrive with more compassion and joy in future situations.

2. Just for today, do not worry.

Worry encourages us to repeatedly think about or try to manipulate situations that are beyond our control. It can leave us feeling increasingly reactive, helpless, inadequate, and negative. Blaming and accusing can also blind us to opportunities where our actions could actually make a difference, further compounding our original worries.

It is possible to respond effectively to situations that concern us. We can take action in the areas of our lives over which we have influence. By creating a positive attitude that ripples out, we benefit the people immediately around us and enhance our surroundings by freeing others to also contribute to positive change.

Taking more responsibility for our own well-being and actions allows us to become more positive and pro-active, especially in situations that involve other people. It is immensely freeing. Over time, even our most tentative but resolute steps away from worry can evolve into the freedom to live in the present moment with appreciation and gratitude.

3. Just for today, I will live in gratitude. I will honour myself, my parents, my elders, and my teachers.

By practicing gratitude, we can grow into appreciation and respect for our own and others' life journeys. It allows us to value the lives, the experiences and the lessons of those who have journeyed before us and have contributed to our growth.

Sometimes, our growth shows up as challenges. However, instead of feeling the isolation of anger and worry, we can feel compassion and gratitude for everyone and everything, as well as their roles in existence. We can invite ourselves to feel interconnected to everything, the whole of life and all its parts.

As we are better able to remain in the awareness of the present moment, we can each find our own beautiful place in the web of life.

4. Just for today, I will earn my living honestly.

We are invited to live and earn our living with a sense of integrity and accountability. Our outer work includes the tasks and services we carry out for others. Our inner work includes taking responsibility for our thoughts, attitudes, and vibrations.

We can begin this work by observing ourselves in terms of our physical sensations, emotional states, needs, thoughts, and spiritual aspirations. Various meditation methods, including Reiki meditation, can be useful in this process. The more we observe and come to know ourselves, the more compassion we develop for ourselves and others. With greater compassion, we are more able to contribute harmoniously to the web of relationships that make up our world.

5. Just for today, I will be kind to every living thing.

The kindness we develop for ourselves and other people can also be offered to our pets, the plants in our gardens, other animals and the forests around us. Eventually the humane, balanced and compassionate treatment of all people, plants and animals becomes natural.

The compassion we offer ourselves can become an outwardly-directed kindness that benefits our world, providing respect for life-bearing earth, air, and water.

The Training Process

Usui Reiki Attunements

The ability to do Reiki is passed on during an attunement. The attunement opens the *Crown, Heart and Palm* chakras to create a special link between the student and the Reiki energy. It aligns and awakens the student's ever-present energy, initiating their ability to access universal energy through the intention to do so.

During the attunement, the student remains seated. While sitting up straight with eyes closed, feet flat on the floor, and palms together over the heart (in a prayer, namaste or gasshô position), the student is guided through some gentle movements by the Reiki Master. Along with touch, the Reiki Master uses breath to "power up" beforehand and then to send energy to the student.

On all levels, the Reiki attunement is a powerful experience. It can open the third eye, increase intuitive awareness, and psychic abilities. The attunement can also start a realignment process that affects the physical body, mind, and emotions. Toxins that have been stored in the body may be released along with feelings and thought patterns that are no longer useful.

Most importantly, the Reiki attunement creates a newfound ability that can never be lost, though the capacity to channel Reiki can always be improved with continued practice. After the attunement, Reiki will flow when the attuned person places his hands on a being with the intention of working towards their highest good.

Some individuals are born with the ability to promote and balance other people's energy with the universal flow. They do not need an attunement to have energy flow through their hands. However, Reiki attunements will enhance their abilities by further clearing and improving their already open channels. People with previous experience doing energy work, consistently report an increase in the strength of their abilities after the Reiki training.

Energetic Realignment

After each level of Reiki attunement, we may experience up to twenty-one days of energetic realignment on the physical, mental, emotional and spiritual levels. This is similar to the effects of a Reiki treatment.

In addition to realigning our energy, an attunement will increase our vibrational capacity and balance our existing energy pathways. The expressions of our energy (thoughts, words, actions, habits, traits, and overall health) become aligned with our highest good as Reiki identifies and strengthens the natural flow of our energy.

Since all aspects of our being are intimately connected, we might experience this energetic shift on a physical or emotional level, so it is important to allow a period of adjustment. On a physical level, we can nurture ourselves with rest, a healthy diet, and an abundance of water. We can also support our emotional health by allowing undiscovered or unwanted emotions to surface and be free. Helpful practices towards a more deeply balanced state could include meditation, journaling, artwork and of course, regular Reiki self-treatments.

The Levels of Usui Reiki

The Usui Reiki System consists of three or four levels. At each level an attunement is given. A Reiki attunement does not create a living being's energy channels; rather, it cleanses and strengthens the naturally-existing channels. Reiki energy is very subtle. It usually takes some time after the first attunement for us to tune in to the energy and appreciate it fully. With each attunement, the major energy centres of the body, called the chakras, are tuned to a higher frequency.

Level I

We receive a permanent attunement that will cleanse and strengthen our chakras to allow us to channel Reiki through the laying on of hands. The First Level is the foundation of all three levels and must be mastered thoroughly before we can be considered ready for the next level.

There is no required period of time before moving on to the next level. Some Reiki associations recommend a number of documented treatments before continuing on to the next level, since practice strengthens and integrates our minds, breath and hands. We become consciously aware of the typical sensations and impressions that occur during a Reiki treatment.

Level II

We are taught three sacred symbols and are attuned to each of them. Our connection to the Reiki energy is strengthened. The symbols are powerful tools of personal discovery, and their integration can benefit others and ourselves. Through these symbols, we learn to increase the focus of the Reiki energy, bring mental and emotional issues to the surface, and send Reiki through time and space. The effective channelling ability is enhanced at this level. Again, it is recommended by some associations that a number of treatments be documented before advancing to the next level.

The Reiki Master/Practitioner Level

We are attuned to the *Usui Master Symbol*, which strengthens our connection to the divine source. We learn a master meditation, practice some advanced energy techniques, and work with crystals. Once again, some associations recommend documented treatments to complete this level.

The Reiki Master/Teacher Level

We fulfill all the requirements and learn all the information and techniques of the Master/Practitioner Level. In addition, we are attuned to three more symbols, learn the technique for giving attunements, and discuss the values and ethics of a Reiki Master/Teacher. This level is for those who have a high level of commitment and desire to teach Reiki to others.

Training Timeline

Level I

8 hour training

Documented treatments as required by your Reiki association

3 month integration time suggested before Level II

Level II

8 hour training

Documented treatments as required by your Reiki association

6 month integration time suggested before Master Levels

Master/Practitioner Level

5 lessons, 2 hours each

Documented treatments as required by your Reiki association

Master/Teacher Level

10 lessons, 2 hours each

Documented treatments as required by your Reiki association

Usui Reiki Technique

The Reiki Session

For a Reiki session to be delightful and helpful, the key is in our attitude. Our intent is for Reiki to flow, without making demands or holding expectations. With our intention, we call on the Reiki energy and are open to it doing whatever is necessary.

Reiki promotes the flow of the universal life force. It can be described as helping to balance a recipient's energy, allowing them to move toward and stay in a more harmonious state. Reiki is one of the few alternative techniques in which the person giving a treatment is also receiving a treatment. As channels of Reiki, we also benefit and may feel energised after giving a Reiki treatment. All those who begin their sessions grounded in Reiki will leave a session with an increased sense of energy and well-being.

We can give Reiki to ourselves or others while engaged in the activities of everyday life. It is a tool for use at any time, in any situation, or in any place for on-the-spot stress release, pain relief, and quick energy. We can use it while waiting in line, preparing dinner, sitting in a dentist's chair, or together with first aid. We can also use Reiki in the heat of an argument or when managing an emergency. Its benefit is immediate and open to all ages. Reiki is always helpful.

A Reiki session can be described as being a combination of deep sleep and awareness. A full treatment lasts between one hour and one and a half hours. However, when there is a shortage of time, shorter sessions can be given with great benefit.

Giving Reiki treatments to ourselves is one of the most important uses of our new ability. Our capacity to channel Reiki gets a little stronger every time we invite it to flow; it is like exercising a muscle. Regular self-treatments are balancing and grounding. Self-treatments enhance our development on all levels, which consequently benefits all those we meet.

Reiki Energy Flow

Although standard hand positions guide the placement of a practitioner's hands, the practitioner does not direct the Reiki. Reiki is guided by universal intelligence. As the practitioner's capacity to step beyond ego develops, so does their ability to channel openly for the recipient. The best results are achieved by remaining relaxed, inviting the energy to flow, with our intent directed towards the highest good of the recipient.

The Reiki energy enters each of us through the crown, the feet, and the base of the spine. From there, it flows to the heart, along the arms and out the palms of the hands to the recipient. When giving Reiki, each hand should be cupped, bringing the thumb along side the fingers. This balances the energy flowing from our hands and keeps it focused on the recipient.

Staying focused on the sensations in our hands will help guide us through the treatment. Reiki is usually felt as warmth or tingling; however, some people feel cold or heaviness in their hands. It is important to focus on any change in sensation since it is our cue about the activity of Reiki. We will also find it useful to scan the recipient's body to determine the best location for the position of our hands. A combination of scanning, intuition, and the standard hand positions can help us proceed in a Reiki session.

In a typical session, our hands will remain in one location for approximately three to five minutes. As we continue to practice, we will notice the energy increase in strength for a certain period and then begin to decline. When we feel the energy subside, we can move our hands to a new position. Instead of breaking contact and moving both hands at the same time, slowly move one hand to a new position and wait a moment to allow the energy flow to resume. Then, slowly bring the other hand alongside.

Sometimes, sensing a strong flow of energy will prompt us to stay in one location for twenty minutes or longer. Then again, we might not sense any flow of energy. In this situation, we stay grounded, and continue thanking Reiki for flowing. After three to five minutes, we can move to the next position. Wherever our hands may be, we are always treating the whole person. The energy will find its own way to where it is needed most, flooding both practitioner and recipient with relaxation and a sense of well-being.

Preparation for a Reiki Session

Preparing Yourself

Before a treatment, prepare yourself by getting centred and using the grounding breath. (See next section)

Preparing the Space

A clean and comfortable atmosphere in the treatment room helps promote a sense of relaxation and trust in the recipient. The following activities can be helpful:

- Playing gentle music in the background.

- Using soft lighting and candles.

- Energetically clearing the treatment table after each treatment.

- Physically or energetically washing your hands before and after treatments.

Preparing the Recipient

Being attentive to the recipient's needs, physical and emotional, supports the recipient in opening up to receive Reiki. Prepare your recipient by asking about their wishes for the treatment. If it is their first Reiki session, they may have questions about the process. Do your best to listen and respond honestly.

You can also take measures that will allow the Reiki energy to flow more freely through both you and the recipient.

- Take off any accessories, such as rings and watches.

- Turn off cell phones and put them aside.

- You and the recipient should be dressed comfortably and avoid tight clothing. The recipient may loosen any articles of tight clothing, such as belts or ties.

Whether the recipient is sitting in a chair or lying down, it is important that they be comfortable.

- If they are lying down, they may appreciate a pillow under their head and knees.

- They may also feel more comfortable with a blanket over their body. Some recipients find, while lying down for an extended period of time, that they start to feel cold.

- Be sure to ask permission before touching a recipient. Remember that Reiki can be given without physical contact.

The Grounding Breath - *Joshin Kokyû Hô*

When we are giving a Reiki treatment, it is essential to be conscious of our breathing; this helps us move out of our intellect and into the flow of Reiki. The breath is the vehicle between the body and the Universe, and the energy, the *ki*, is the passenger.

Sensei Usui taught his students a breathing technique called *Jôshin Kokyû Hô*, which translates roughly into English as "the breathing method for cleansing the spirit." (Refer to Bronwen and Frans Stiene's book "*The Japanese Art of Reiki*" for more detailed information.)

As taught by Sensei Usui, the technique is done in the following manner:

1. Sit comfortably, keeping your spine as straight as possible without becoming tense.

2. Inhaling slowly through your nose, draw your breath far down into your belly. Be aware of your muscles all the way down to your pelvic area to help you bring your breath to the energy centre located two or three finger widths below your navel (*Sacral or Second Chakra*).

3. With each breath, imagine yourself inviting, not only air, but also Reiki energy through the top of your head (*Crown Chakra*). Bring this energy down to the *Sacral Chakra* as well.

4. For a few seconds, hold your breath, and energy, at the *Second Chakra*, to help root the Reiki in your body and its energy pathways.

5. While exhaling, imagine expanding the energy out from your *Second Chakra*, through your body and into the area immediately surrounding you. Visualise yourself filling your aura with Reiki.

This is how we cleanse ourselves and become a clearer channel for Reiki. The energy flows into us from the Universe and back again into the Universe. The cycle is completed.

You may feel directly how the energy enters through the *Crown Chakra*. It may feel like a gentle tingle or a sensation of lightness and warmth.

If you do not feel the energy right away, don't worry, just continue to breathe calmly and serenely. Reiki is always beneficial, and with time, the effect of this exercise will make itself known as a strong and enriching source of energy.

Opening and Closing Protocol

The combination of our attitude and intent starts the Reiki flowing through us. All treatments are begun, conducted and closed with a sense of gratitude and respect. No matter the hand positions used, follow the opening and closing protocol outlined below.

Opening

1. Ground yourself. Standing outside the recipient's energy field, do three *Jôshin Kokyû Hô* breaths to cleanse your energy channels and anchor yourself in the energy of the Universe.

2. While breathing in Reiki, request, "Reiki, please flow."

3. Give gratitude. Thank Reiki for:

   • The time and opportunity for this session, and this powerful and effective energy that is guiding you and the treatment.

   • Sensei Usui, his life, and the lives he has touched.

   • The recipient, their life, and the lives they have touched.

4. Invite, if you feel called to do so, other beings of light or Reiki guides to assist you in the Reiki session.

During the Session

Throughout the session, be mindful of your breathing and reaffirm your gratitude for the presence of Reiki, the sense of well being it brings and the guidance it offers.

Closing

1. When closing the session, say three times: "Seal this healing in light and love".

2. Say: "As it is and so it shall be."

3. On behalf of both of you and the recipient, give thanks for:

   - Sensei Usui, his life and the lives he has touched.

   - The recipient's life and the lives they have touched.

   - Your life and the lives you have touched.

   - The beings of light and guides who may have helped you.

You can also help settle the recipient's energy by sweeping your fingers through the outer area of her energy field. This can be done during the session, but is particularly useful for closing a treatment.

Allow the recipient time to arise slowly after the treatment. They may appreciate a drink of water.

Hand Positions

The basic hand positions offer a well-balanced and universal guide to giving Reiki sessions. Our hands may gently touch the recipient or be a comfortable distance above them (usually about 5cm). Careful and gentle touch is quite important at the head and throat area, and maintaining a distance is particularly important when working around sexual areas or wounds.

We make a special effort to know these basic positions well, even though we will eventually feel the urge to vary the positions or to go directly to an area not included in the standard repertoire. When this happens, we are being guided by the flow of Reiki and our intuition. Stay open to the guidance of the energy itself. This is Reiki in its highest form and it will offer us the most valuable guidance we can have during a session.

Standard hand positions are described in the following sections:

- Quick Self-Treatment

- Full Self-Treatment

- Reiki Chair Session

- Treating a Person on a Massage Table

Although hand positions are connected to certain chakras or parts of the body, Reiki uses these positions to balance the whole person. (For more about the chakras, refer to the chapter on Energy Centres.) It can enter at one point and flow elsewhere as needed. If you follow the hand positions or your intuition to a site of a noticeable imbalance, remember you are bringing Reiki to the whole person, not just a body part.

Quick Self-Treatment

Using your breath, focus your intent.

Follow the opening protocol.

Hand Positions:

1. Place both hands together between your eyebrows (*Third Eye Chakra*)

2. Move one hand to the nape of your neck

3. Moving hands one at a time, place both hands on any other part of your body where you want to benefit from Reiki

Close with gratitude and follow the closing protocol.

Full Self-Treatment

Using your breath, focus your intent.

Follow the opening protocol.

Place and slowly move your hands:

1. Together on your eyes and face (*Third Eye Chakra*)

2. Over your ears

3. On the crown of your head (*Crown Chakra*)

4. Side by side on the back of your head

5. On your shoulders

6. Over your throat (*Throat Chakra*)

7. With one hand on the throat, and the other over the centre of your chest (*Throat and Heart Chakras*)

8. On the top of your abdomen along your lowest ribs (*Solar Plexus Chakra*)

9. On the middle of your abdomen (*Sacral Chakra*)

10. The bottom of your abdomen at the pubic bone (*Root Chakra*)

11. On the middle of your back below your ribs (*Sacral Chakra*)

12. On the lower back at the tailbone (*Root Chakra*)

13. On your thighs

14. On your knees

15. On your feet, or beamed to your feet, to create flow throughout your entire system

Close in gratitude and follow the closing protocol.

Reiki Chair Session

Reiki can be given to a person while they are comfortably seated in a chair. The recipient may be sitting normally in a chair, may be nearly horizontal and facing up in a recliner, or may be face down on a massage chair with their body at a 45° angle. How a person is seated will affect how you position your hands. The next section, *Treating a Person on a Massage Table*, outlines the hand positions for a practitioner who is giving a treatment to a person who is lying face up, typically on a massage table. You can use the same hand positions that are outlined in the next section, modifying them as the seating arrangement requires.

Treating a Person on a Massage Table

After making the recipient comfortable, ask, "Is there anything specific you want to address during this session?"

Using your breath, focus your intent.

Place your hands:

1. Across the chest, focusing on gratitude (*Heart Chakra*)

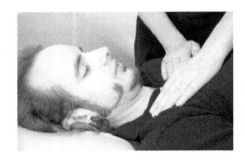

2. Around the head and throat:

   a. On top of the eyes and forehead while standing behind the recipient's head (*Third Eye Chakra*)

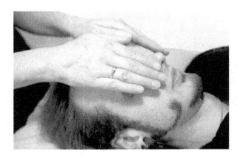

   b. Cupped around the ears

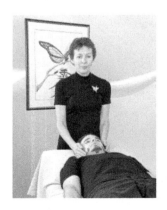

c. Behind the head

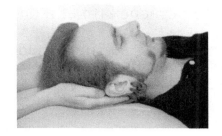

d. Cupped below the chin, fingertips touching over the throat (*Throat Chakra*)

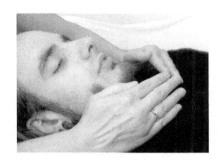

e. Below the throat, with fingertips touching to make a "V" on the chest (*Throat Chakra*)

f. Above the crown of the head, with thumbs and fingers forming a triangle (*Crown Chakra*)

3. On one arm at a time:

    a. The shoulder

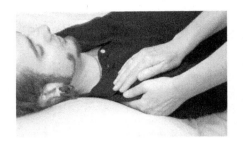

    b. The elbow

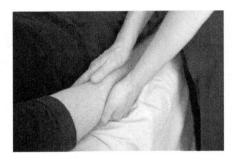

    c. The wrist

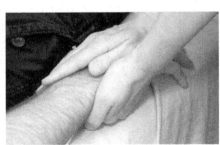

    d. The hand

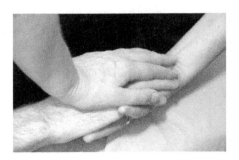

4. Across the abdomen at the bottom of the ribs (*Solar Plexus Chakra*)

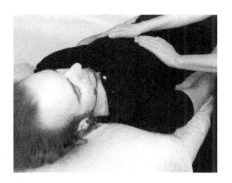

5. On both hips (*Creativity and Root Chakra*)

6. On one leg at a time:

   a. The hip

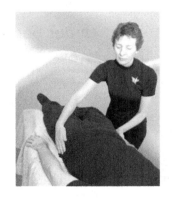

   b. Above and below the knee

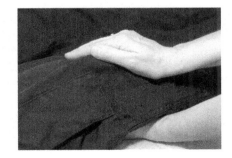

c. Above and below the ankle

d. Under both feet

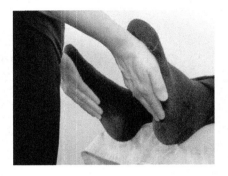

Work back up the other side of the body to the shoulder, before continuing with the following positions.

7. At the chest:

   a. One hand at the top of the chest and the other at the lower ribs (*Heart Chakra and Solar Plexus Chakra*)

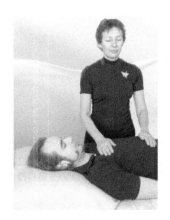

b. In a "T" position over the top of the recipient's chest (*Heart Chakra*) to begin closing the session

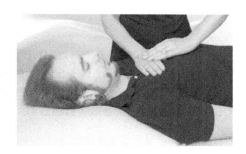

Close in gratitude and follow the closing protocol.

Sweep one of your hands through the edge of the recipient's energy field. Start from about 24" (60 cm) above the head (also known as the "centre above"), sweeping over the torso to about 24" (60 cm) below the feet (also known as the "centre below"), and then back up again in the opposite direction.

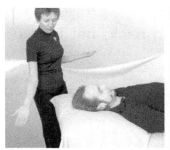

Step about 24" (60 cm) away to remove yourself from the recipient's energy field. Focus on breaking contact with the recipient's energy.

Allow the recipient some time to sit up. They may appreciate some water to drink.

Good Posture

While doing Reiki, we may notice that we can hold our hands out in front of us longer than we normally can. Nonetheless, cultivating a habit of good posture, having our table at an appropriate height, and doing stretches will also help us to be comfortable while giving Reiki sessions.

Posture

Rely on the posturing of your skeletal system, especially your spine, to maintain a beneficial treatment position. If we use our muscles and related tissues to perform the job of the skeleton, we often experience tension or knots. We will be much more comfortable if we remain mindful of how our bodies are positioned in relation to the spine and skeletal system. You can help yourself do this by:

- Keeping your centre of balance, not maintaining a position that tilts or leans

- Relaxing your shoulders so they are down and back, not held up towards your ears

- Moderating the amount of time spent at any one location, as even the strongest muscles will get tired

Table Height

Set the table so your posture can remain upright while holding your hands over the recipient. Although your arms are outstretched, allow them to drop comfortably from your shoulders with a relaxed bend at the elbows; your shoulders should be back and down. The optimal height of your table is determined by your height and the size/girth of the person you are treating.

Stretching

Stretching before and after a Reiki session can help increase your comfort during treatments. Stretching can also help improve flexibility, as well as overall joint and muscle health. Gentleness is key; increase the tension in a stretch until you feel "comfortably uncomfortable." Yoga and Pilates instructors, athletic trainers, physiotherapists and ergonomic specialists can provide excellent stretches.

Energy Centres

Major Energy Centres: The Chakras

The chakras are the major energy centres of the non-physical, energy body. Each centre is associated with specific spiritual, emotional and physical conditions. The seven major chakra centres are described below.

First or *Root Chakra* (red)
Located at the base of the spine. Associated with groundedness, security and the ability to deal with day-to-day life; it is linked to the adrenal glands.

Second or *Sacral Chakra* (orange)
Located just below the navel. It is the centre for creativity, vitality, sensuality and sexuality; it is linked to the ovaries and testicles.

Third or *Solar Plexus Chakra* (yellow)
Located in the abdomen below the ribs. It is associated with will, self-esteem and personal power; it is linked to the pancreas.

Fourth or *Heart Chakra* (green)
Located in the centre of the chest at the level of the physical heart. It is associated with love and compassion; it is linked to the thymus.

Fifth or *Throat Chakra* (light blue)
Located at the throat. It is associated with creative expression, speaking the truth, communication and openness; it is linked to the thyroid.

Sixth or *Third Eye Chakra* (indigo)
Located between the eyebrows. It is associated with intuition, creative thinking and psychic abilities; it is linked to the pituitary gland.

Seventh or *Crown Chakra* (mauve)

Located at the top of the head. It is connected to spiritual consciousness, oneness with all cosmic understanding; it is linked to the pineal gland.

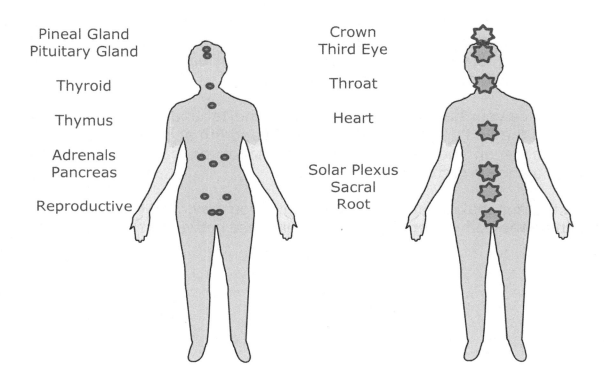

Pineal Gland
Pituitary Gland

Thyroid

Thymus

Adrenals
Pancreas

Reproductive

Crown
Third Eye

Throat

Heart

Solar Plexus
Sacral
Root

Chakra Balancing

When a chakra centre is out of balance, it can cause problems in the areas to which it is linked. There are many methods of using Reiki to balance the chakras. Two are listed below:

- Place one hand on the *Crown Chakra* for the duration of the treatment. The other hand is used to balance each progressive chakra, starting with the *Third Eye*. Treat each chakra with Reiki until balance is restored.

- Place your hands simultaneously on the 1st and 7th chakras, then on the 2nd and 6th, next on the 3rd and 5th and ending with both hands on the heart. Leave your hands on each position until balance is restored.

Note that for chakra balancing treatments, you may need to treat without touching the body where the physical distance between the hands is too great.

Paperwork

Associations, Legal Issues and Record Keeping

Being a member of your local Reiki association encourages the promotion of ethical practices and educational standards, and could provide the public with referrals for practitioners and teachers. (Refer to the Appendix for Reiki association websites).

Most Reiki associations provide a code of ethics, which clearly outlines appropriate record keeping and conduct for all members who practice Reiki.

It is very important to gain consent from the recipient before you give Reiki. It is also important to never interfere with the advice or treatment of a licensed medical professional. In particular, never suggest the recipient stop taking prescription medication. It is entirely the recipient's choice to make such a decision.

We can say that Reiki is used for stress reduction and relaxation. It is important not to make any claims for physical or psychological cures.

As a practitioner, or a student preparing to become a practitioner, client information must be kept confidential and up to date. The forms on the following two pages are examples of a client information form/waiver and an ongoing treatment log.

Client Information Form

Use a current client information form approved by your Reiki association. Alternatively, you may use the following format to create your own.

Begin with a statement that includes:
- Reiki is used for stress reduction and to help promote relaxation
- Practitioner does not diagnose nor prescribe
- Practitioner will not interfere with a treatment protocol of a licensed medical professional
- For any physical or psychological conditions, see a licensed medical professional

Name: _____ E-mail: _____

Address: _____ City: _____

Province: _____ Postal Code: _____ Phone: _____

Are you currently under the care of your family physician or specialist?
Yes ____ No ____

If yes, please elaborate: _____

Are you currently taking any medications?   Yes ____   No ____

If yes, please elaborate: _____

Are you currently receiving other treatments?   Yes ____   No ____

If yes, please elaborate: _____

Do you or have you suffered from seizures of any sort?   Yes ____   No ____

If yes, please elaborate: _____

Are you comfortable with being touched during the Reiki session or would you prefer to not be touched?   Yes, touch is OK ____   No, do not touch ____

Signed: _____ Date: _____

Treatment Log

Recipient's Name: _____   Date of Session: _____

Comments:

Recipient's Name: _____   Date of Session: _____

Comments:

Recipient's Name: _____   Date of Session: _____

Comments:

Impressions

As part of your Level I training, you will experience Reiki as both the recipient and the practitioner. You are invited to record your impressions here.

Receiving a Reiki Treatment:

Giving a Reiki Treatment:

Appendix

Bibliography

Brennan, Barbara Ann. *Hands of Light*. New York: Bantam Books, 1988.

Honervogt, Tanmaya. *The Power of Reiki, An Ancient Hands-on Healing Technique.* New York: Henry Holt and Company, 1998.

Kelly, Maureen. *Reiki and the Healing Buddha.* Wisconsin: Lotus Press, 2000.

Petter, Frank Arjava. *Reiki Fire.* Wisconsin: Lotus Press, 2008.

Petter, Frank Arjava and Lubeck, Walter and Rand, William Lee. *The Spirit of Reiki,* Wisconsin: Lotus Press, 2009.

Petter, Frank Arjava and Usui, Dr. Mikao. *The Original Handbook of Dr. Mikao Usui.* Wisconsin: Lotus Press, 2000.

Rand, William Lee. *Reiki: The Healing Touch First & Second Level Manual.* Minnesota: Vision Publications, 2000 (MI).

Rand, William Lee. *The Reiki Touch.* Sounds True; Spi edition. 2006.

Stein, Diane. *Essential Reiki*. California: The Crossing Press, 1995.

Stiene, Bronwen and Frans. *The Japanese Art of Reiki.* Hants, UK: O Books, 2005.

Stiene, Bronwen and Frans. *The Reiki Sourcebooki.* Hants, UK: O Books, 2010.

Recommended Websites

Reiki Associates: www.reikiassociates.com

Canadian Reiki Association: www.Reiki.ca

World Reiki Association: www.worldreikiassociation.org

The Reiki Association (UK): www.reikiassociation.org.uk

Made in the USA
Las Vegas, NV
01 September 2021